SUPERNAT

DARLINGTON

True Ghostly Encounters

Sylvia Clement

First Printing: 2019

supernaturaldarlington@gmail.com

> "The supernatural is the natural not yet understood."
>
> –Elbert Hubbard

In loving memory of

Elizabeth Eleanor Noble

1935-2019

Table of Contents

ACKNOWLEDGEMENTS xi

FOREWORD...xii

THE WATCHED 1

THE SLOT MACHINE GHOST 1

SHADOWS 2

WALKING THROUGH WALLS..2

THE SEATED GHOST...2

FIGURE OF A NURSE...3

FOOTSTEPS ON THE STAIRS..3

CELLAR MAN 4

A LOVELY WARM GLOW 4

LADY IN A BALL GOWN 5

VICTORIAN CHAMBER MAID...5

WEIRD VIBE..5

SMASHED CUP 6

THE HAUNTED BUS COMPANY 6

A CONFUSED LITTLE SPIRIT BOY 7

TOP HAT AND CANE...8

THE CASE OF THE DISAPPEARING BARMAN.............................9

A LITTLE UNEASY 10

CONVERSING WITH THE DEAD 10

WATCHING THE WATCHERS 11

IMAGES FROM THE PAST 12

FLYING GLASSES AND DEBAUCHARY 12

A MYSTERIOUS MONK 13

A MYSTERIOUS MONK AGAIN 13

THEME BAR HAUNTING... 14

SUNDAY AT THE WEST CEMETERY 15

A DISEMBODIED HEAD 19

STORED BODIES 19

LADY AT THE JUNCTION 20

WEIRD THINGS 20

FLOATING WOMAN AND THE MOVING CHAIR................ 20

THEY ALL FLOAT.. 21

THE HAUNTED ONES 22

MISCHEVIOUS GHOST BOY.................................... 22

WAKEY, WAKEY 23

WAKEY, WAKEY THREE DOORS AWAY 24

A LIFE DRAINING HOUSE 25

SPIRIT BOY OF THE RIVER SKERNE...................... 25

SOMETHING EVIL 26

MIRROR SPIRIT 26

GHOST CAT... 27

HELD BY AN UNKNOWN FORCE 28

MY NIGHT VISITOR 28

UNWANTED VISITOR 28

DISAPPEARING LADY IN THE NIGHT 29

A SCARY FEELING 29

LAUGHTER AND SNEEZING 30

ROTTING FISH 30

THE LADY IN RED 31

LADY IN RED AGAIN 34

GHOST ON THE BRIDGE 35

DARK FIGURE 35

A SPOOKY MISUNDERSTANDING 35

HEAD IN THE GAS OVEN 36

NOISES IN THE ATTIC 37

SHADOW CHILD 37

VICTORIAN LADY IN THE 21ST CENTURY 38

WHITE SOCKS 38

A FADING WOMAN 39

TINKLING IVORIES 40

TOP HAT AND TAILS 40

ROAMING THE BEDROOMS 41

OLD WOMAN AT THE WINDOW 41

ALL HALLOWS' EVE IN A CEMETERY 42

SUICIDE MAID 43

A BABY'S CRY 44

ELIZABETHAN GHOST? 44

WHO PUT THE LIGHT ON? 44

HAUNTED TWIN 45

ROTTING FLESH 49

TOO SCARED TO GO TO SLEEP...49

TRESPASSER OR GHOST?...50

FREAKED OUT 50

LIGHT A CANDLE AND SAY A PRAYER 51

SPOOKY GOINGS ON 51

NOT THE ONLY ONE LIVING HERE 52

NEW YEAR'S EVE FRIGHT NIGHT......................................53

VICTORIAN CHILD WITH THE FAKE SMILE 54

TERRIFYING THE BABYSITTERS 54

SO ANGRY...56

FACE AT THE WINDOW 57

PADFOOT 58

FEVER HOUSE...59

SEVEN OF SPADES 62

WET WOOLY GLOVES..63

UNSOCIABLE SPIRITS 64

GHOST SOLDIER ON THE STAIRS 65

RELEASED..65

SPOOKY BASEMENT...66

NON-BELIEVER...66

RING, RING..66

SPOOKY SHIFTS..67

ABOUT THE AUTHOR...72

ACKNOWLEDGEMENTS

I have to start by thanking my husband John and family for their awesome support during the process of creating this book. Also, thank you to Julian L Harrop from Beamish Museum for allowing me to use the Raby Hotel image. I would also like to express my gratitude to Janet Melody for designing the front page graphics and Beryl Hankin for inspiring me to begin this project. Finally, I am extremely grateful to the residents of Darlington for sharing their stories and making this book possible.

Sylvia Clement 2019

FOREWORD

D o ghosts exist, or are they a figment of the imagination? How many of us have had such experiences yet never told the tale? This is the question I first posed on social media in 2013. In response to my query, hundreds of residents flocked to share their tales. Now I wish to share those experiences with a wider audience.

The tales I have compiled for you are some of the strangest and spookiest I have read so far. My personal favourites are "The Lady in Red," "Old Woman at the Window," and "Ghost Soldier on the Stairs." But there are many more!

In addition, this book is a lasting testimony of tales that may have been otherwise forgotten. I have altered none, although I have omitted the exact locations and names of contributors to preserve privacy. I have, however, kept a full record for future reference.

I must sign off now so you can begin this supernatural journey of Darlington dear reader. But before I do, I must warn you! Don't read this book late at night or on your own. It's far too scary!

Sylvia Clement 2019

THE WATCHED

I work in a shop on Bondgate, and it's safe to say that no one likes to go to the top floor alone. It's not a nice feeling at all, it's so creepy. When I worked at Past Times on High Row, we had a spirit but it was a nice feeling, kind of made you feel at home. I often worked there on my own and was quite content. But in this place I don't even like to go in there alone.

I also work there. The top floor definitely feels different to anywhere else in the building. You feel watched...

THE SLOT MACHINE GHOST

I was shopping in town one summer morning in 2015 and called into a betting shop to place my usual bet. As I was choosing a slip, I happened to glance up and saw the hunched figure of a man sitting at a slot machine by the door. Then, all of a sudden he disappeared! Not believing what I had just seen I asked the assistant if she had noticed anything. After describing the apparition, the assistant said she had also seen the same figure on many occasions!

SHADOWS

My mam used to work at a shoe shop on Bondgate. There was such a horrible feeling in the place, especially the upstairs staff room area. The dark corridor where stock was kept was creepy too. I was once in the staff room and heard footsteps coming up the stairs but there was no one there. I never actually saw anything. It was more the feeling of the place, as though you're not alone. I know other people have experienced things there such as seeing shadows and hearing noises. I remember feeling terrified upstairs if I was on my own.

WALKING THROUGH WALLS

Has anyone ever had a spooky experience in Abbott's Yard to the rear of the Art Shop? My mam was going to walk through there but waited for a man to come out. He came from Bondgate, turned right and then vanished into the wall!

THE SEATED GHOST

The Civic Theatre (now The Hippodrome) is well known for its many hauntings. There are several ghosts; the latest caught on camera in 2016! A tour guide I spoke with said that one day a cleaner got a fright as chair HH13 was down (as if someone was sat on it.) There is no way you could get the chair to stay down as they are spring loaded! Also, the phone upstairs would ring downstairs, but everyone knew nobody was upstairs!

FIGURE OF A NURSE

My wife used to work at Beaumont House in Darlington when the RAC call centre was based there. I believe it's built on the site of an old hospital. There were stories of people doing late shift and seeing a figure of a nurse crossing the floor!

FOOTSTEPS ON THE STAIRS

My friend and I used to have a shop called The Forest Path in Buckton's Yard, Darlington. I've had one creepy experience there, as had my friend. My experience was when we were doing an EVP in the upper levels of the building. A group of people were there with us, but all had reason to go downstairs and outside, leaving me on the first floor. We'd been conducting the EVP on the second floor.

It was a shamble of a room, very large, covering the length of Buckton's Yard and going across the top of all the shops. The first floor was only one room which housed the door to the stairs and the second floor and a small dilapidated toilet. I was about to go downstairs when I heard footsteps as clear as day coming down from the second floor. I tried to keep my nerve and see what was going to come round the corner. But to my shame, as the footsteps reached the last few steps, I left sharpish!

CELLAR MAN

My twin brother had an encounter with the supernatural in a cafe on Crown Street. He had been to the toilet looked down the cellar to see a man stood in a white coat looking up at him which triggered his instinct to run screaming!

A LOVELY WARM GLOW

I would have been a young teenager sitting in the adult end of Darlington Library about thirty years ago. I was reading a book and looked up to see into the window in the building opposite. The room inside looked rather grand. There was an open coal fire, well stocked, giving a lovely warm glow and a portrait hanging on the wall. I remember thinking it looked so inviting. I glanced back to my book and remembered the building was closed! I looked back up, and it was just a window. I could not even see in it as it was empty. It did not frighten me; I just felt a bit sad as it was not there when I looked again. It was the old mill, closed now unfortunately pulled down to make room for the not so beautiful car park.

Was it my imagination as a young girl? I do not know, but I thought I would tell my little story to ask if anyone else had seen it?

LADY IN A BALL GOWN

Can anyone remember the story or have you seen the lady in a ball gown looking into the river at Stone Bridge?

VICTORIAN CHAMBER MAID

I worked in a hotel on Victoria Road. Other people who worked there experienced strange things like kettles turning themselves on. The building dates back to the 1870s and I'm intrigued by it. It used to be the North Eastern Hotel and belonged to the railway. Workers have often seen a Victorian chamber maid carrying a tray down the staircase. She appears down in the basement too, in a room that looks like it was a kitchen all those years ago.

WEIRD VIBE

A mate's house on Uplands Road has a weird vibe in the attic bedroom. One time, the room filled with the smell of pipe tobacco. As far as I am aware, nobody smoked. Well, certainly not in that house!

SMASHED CUP

When a mere youth I used to work at Fine Fare on Northgate. We had a few strange happenings in that place. I remember one. Never worried about ghosts, I wandered alone up to the warehouse and looked in the canteen. There was nothing to see. So I thought I would go to the top end and was about fifteen yards down the warehouse when I heard a smash from the canteen. I rushed back to look, and in the middle of the room was a smashed cup. It was about six feet from any of the tables and sink.

Another time, a member of staff was opening up the shop early one morning. The moment he entered, the lights came on by themselves. This was a feat in itself, as there were about four banks of ten switches! After that day he would not go into the shop on his own, despite his black belt in karate!

THE HAUNTED BUS COMPANY

My dad was the building manager responsible for every building United owned. He was responsible for answering the alarms at the head office and would go in the dead of night. One of the old buildings was a former convent and was beautiful inside. I often used to go with my dad, but it was a horrid place. One night he got a call, grabbed our Alsatian as he always did and set off for the offices. Once there, dad checked the alarm panel. He found that the zone triggered some doors right next to the cellar. When he went to investigate the Alsatian stood rigid and howled the place down, refusing to go any further. He let go of her leader and went himself. When he arrived, he was immediately frozen as he could hear screaming from the cellar and the sounds of a child in distress!

This happened to him a few times over the years and was glad when they finally re-located to Morton Park. Also, the staff toilets upstairs were spooky. Women refused to go in there on their own as things would move and doors would slam. It was a massive place mind, and I used to love exploring it out of hours when my dad was there for some reason. You could go right out the back to where the buses were being fixed and even into the air-raid shelters too.

A CONFUSED LITTLE SPIRIT BOY

My mam works in a charity shop in town and it's rife with activity including sightings of a little boy. Also, lots of things vanish and are then found in ridiculous places. A woman who got the manager's job only lasted one day. She posted the keys through the assistant manager's door with a note saying I won't be returning. Later they spoke to her, and she told them the place was so evil she couldn't stand it. And that something terrible had happened to the little boy. A clairvoyant, who was brought in, told a volunteer that the little boy who plays on the stairs is confused as there are no doors. All the doors have been blocked off, so only door frames remain.

Also, there is the feeling that something is there when alone, such as seeing movements out of the corner of your eye. The stairs leading up to the top floor and the wall is freezing. There is a heavy feeling on the stairs the little boy plays on. Three people have mentioned a little boy, so I am certain he's there and whether there is something else not so nice I don't know.

My wife works as a volunteer at the same charity shop. She tells me that the ghost of a young boy haunts the place. Some staff don't like being upstairs in the shop alone. And on occasions things have been moved or mislaid. Does anybody know more about this ghost?

TOP HAT AND CANE

I originated from Shropshire and lived in a village that had lots of ghosts, some seen by my parents and sister. I once saw a ghost whilst working at an RAF base in Lincolnshire. I moved to Darlington ten years ago, and the only spirit I have seen was about six years ago. It was in a coffee shop on Post House Wynd. I took my young daughter to the ladies upstairs, and it was freezing cold. I also felt a sense of panic and anxiety when I was up there. As we came out of the door, I saw a man with a top hat, a big black moustache, a cape and a cane in his hand. Not wanting to panic my daughter, I shut the door. Then when I opened it again, he was gone! I was like Linford Christie going down those stairs and told my husband what I saw. I also mentioned it to the staff on leaving. I've never been again!

THE CASE OF THE DISAPPEARING BARMAN

About ten years ago we were on a works night out in a re-vamped night club and were the first to arrive. I was also the first one at the little bar in the club. The man behind the bar who was in his fifties with silver-grey hair and a white shirt asked for my order.

So I said, "Two pints of lager."

I then saw him walk into the back room. Then two young people appeared and started serving. The club was now getting busy. Five minutes later, I asked the young chap that I was still waiting for my drinks.

The young guy said, "I don't recall serving you?"

I said, "No, the older gent did, he went into the back room."

The young guy said, "There is no older gent here. We are the only two serving tonight at this bar."

I said, "He is in the back room. I saw him walk in."

The young guy looked back into the stockroom and said, "There is no one in there and there is no way out of that room."

I returned to my friends.

My mate said, "What's wrong with you? You look like you've seen a ghost!"

A LITTLE UNEASY

I work at a restaurant in Darlington town centre opposite some empty offices that was once a house. One morning I went into work about 6.30 am as I needed to finish cleaning and get away to do some shopping. I was working at the front of the restaurant when I looked across and noticed a lady in the window downstairs in the empty offices. She was just standing there, looking out. My first thought was that she might be showing someone around. So I looked away and was about to plug in the vacuum cleaner when I looked again and she was in the upstairs window. There was no way she could have got upstairs so quickly! To say I was a little uneasy is an understatement. And then she disappeared! I don't know to this day if I saw a real person or not!

CONVERSING WITH THE DEAD

My brother told me this. He and his girlfriend were on High Row talking to a friend of theirs. The same evening, they went to Croft for a drink and mentioned in conversation that they were speaking to this mutual friend. The people were dumbfounded and explained he had died a week ago! My brother didn't know he had died and so was doubly shocked!

WATCHING THE WATCHERS

I'm certain I saw a ghost in a Darlington cinema a few years ago. I took my son and his three friends to see a film and we were the only ones in screen downstairs. It was a foggy November night, and the cinema was quiet. During the film I turned to look behind and saw a tall man, dressed all in black, standing still and watching us. I couldn't make out any features as the whole figure was so black. He didn't move or make any gestures. He wore a long jacket and a hat. I remember thinking that it was unusual clothing-Victorian, perhaps. Nothing like the uniform that the staff was wearing. Then he saw me looking. So he turned and drifted up the aisle towards the doors at the top and disappeared. There was no sound of the doors opening or closing, but he was no longer in the room. This puzzled me. So I got out of my seat and walked up the aisle to find out what I had seen. Yet there was nobody in sight. There was no staff at all and no one in the toilets. I didn't want to scare the kids, so I didn't speak to the staff when the film finished.

A few months later, I returned and discussed my experience with members of staff. I found out I wasn't the only one who had seen this figure as other people had reported seeing similar happenings.

IMAGES FROM THE PAST

Is anyone interested in ghosts and images from the past? Ghosts are just images from the past showing through. At the back of Pease's cemetery I've walked up and down there on a night for nearly twenty years, all hours, early and late with my dog. One night as I was going in my back gate, something inside me said look down the lane. I did, and saw an image of a horse and cart with a man sat at the front of the cart. It was like looking at a negative of a photo. I know what I saw. It was as clear as day. The way it was facing was with the back of the cart facing the cemetery wall!

A couple of days later I stood in the same area and looked at the wall. It was covered in ivy coming to ground level. I moved the ivy over to one side, and low and behold an entrance which was once there had been bricked up. I realised that was where they carried the deceased through! I know what I saw. I don't drink and wasn't on any medication. It didn't scare me. It taught me to be happier to have seen such a thing and have a deeper understanding of the now and then as one day we will just be images for someone else.

FLYING GLASSES AND DEBAUCHARY

I worked at the Tap & Spile where lots of creepy stuff happened. Nobody liked walking past the window upstairs, which looked into a function room. Glasses would fly off shelves. Staff also reported seeing a woman in a green dress. And there was a little boy that haunted the area that's the ladies' toilets. I paid a visit to the library where I found an old newspaper article. The article stated that a council official visited the pub about a licensing issue. But "was so horrified by the debauchery" the pub didn't get an entertainment license for a good while after. This has always amused me.

A MYSTERIOUS MONK

It was a misty night and late. I was walking my dog along by St Cuthbert's Church, when suddenly he ran off. I wandered around to find him. Then, out of nowhere, Patch was barking like a mad dog at a set of steps at the back of the church. While he was still barking, I could see a figure walking down the steps. It looked like a monk in dark clothes. It got to the bottom of the steps then disappeared through the door! I took Patch home sharpish and made myself a strong drink!

A MYSTERIOUS MONK AGAIN

I too had a strange encounter near St Cuthbert's church. It was December about 4 pm and I was in the Market Place sat on the church wall waiting for my friend. As I looked towards the church, I saw a man (dressed in what I can only describe as sackcloth and a hood) walking along the path. He turned to look at me but kept on walking. His face had a green tinge to it. He continued to look at me, and I got a feeling of dread in the pit of my stomach. I was relieved when he turned the corner and I could see him no more.

THEME BAR HAUNTING

After working in a hotel management position in Windsor, I secured a job at a new theme bar in Darlington. This was in the early 90s. I worked there for about five years and had lots of strange experiences there. Working mid week, we closed up after a very slow night. As I cashed up the barman, who will remain nameless, sorted the bar out. When this was all done, we settled down at the end of the bar with a pint and a ciggie (those were the days.) Only the emergency lighting remained on. As we sat and chatted, we heard noises on the second floor, footsteps and the odd knock. We checked every room and knew there was nobody but us there. Bewildered, we decided to investigate and made our way upstairs. As we reached the top step, we heard an almighty crash from the kitchen. I almost soiled myself! Having run back downstairs like a couple of little girls, we retraced our steps. We went into the kitchen and found a whole tray of cutlery scattered across the room. This happened frequently.

Also, one of the supervisors used to open up alone on an evening sometimes. She went in one dark winter's evening at around 6 pm. She set about getting the tills ready as the front doors were still locked. She went up to the second floor behind the upstairs bar to the staff room and toilet. She turned the light on and as she did, the door slammed behind her. Turning she tried to open the door but the handle would not push down. It was as if someone was holding it from the other side. She became very upset and let go. A few seconds later the door clicked open and swung towards her. There was no lock on this door!

Working there as a manager, I didn't have a lot of time in the building on my own. But always felt like there was a presence. I often heard doors banging. It was weird; I felt there was someone in there with me, but I never felt scared. One night I was locking up when I saw a figure standing on the balcony, right next to the upstairs office. It was the figure of a monk. Even after I saw this, I never felt scared being on my own in there. I always felt safe.

SUNDAY AT THE WEST CEMETERY

My hubby and I were at the West Cemetery early one summer morning looking for my ancestor's gravestone. It had rained heavily but started to brighten up. Suddenly there seemed quite a lot of people milling about. A man with an old type coach pram passed us several times as we searched amongst the gravestones. I felt rather uneasy as both the man and the child in the pram were grinning at us like Cheshire cats. Something just didn't feel right. The pair passed again and then the man sat on a bench close by, watching. The bench was wet from the rain and he just carried on sitting there. Rather strange I thought. Next time I looked up they had vanished!

We eventually gave up looking and headed back to the car. As we did so, a woman in black stopped us and asked if we had seen a funeral taking place at the Crematorium as she was late. That seemed strange, as funerals don't take place there on a Sunday. She thanked us, carried on walking towards the Crematorium then we lost sight of her too! I still feel uneasy when I think of that Sunday at the cemetery.

A view of Bondgate taken from the roof terrace of the Majestic.

Entrance to Abbott's Yard.

Darlington Library, Crown Street.

British Heart Foundation, Northgate.

17

Peacocks, was Fine Fare, Northgate.

The Odeon, Northgate.

A DISEMBODIED HEAD

In the 60s I lived at The Raby Hotel on Tubwell Row which is now demolished. As a child I used to converse with the spirit/ghost (temporal echo) of a woman. I can remember one instance when she was sat on the edge of a bed, brushing her long dark hair, wearing a white nightdress. This was in the attic that was once the servant's quarters.

I learned that she had committed suicide due to the mistreatment received by her employer. Also related to this is the manifestation of a head of a man in my parent's bedroom. I remember this well, as it scared the hell out of them. I was present, and it was quite scary for me to see my parents so rattled. What we saw was a manifestation of the owner who had pushed the woman to the extreme course of hanging herself.

STORED BODIES

I live in a flat on North Road that used to be a place where bodies were stored before the funerals many years ago! It feels really spooky in here.

LADY AT THE JUNCTION

Is the cattle market haunted? I went past the other night. I came off Victoria Road and up the hill towards the cattle market. On the corner of the T junction of Waverley Terrace, I saw a woman in an old-fashioned dress with blonde hair; it was long and wavy. She was stood there, and then disappeared! Has anyone else seen her?

WEIRD THINGS

Some very weird things have happened in my parent's house off North Road. I heard from a spiritualist that the streets off North Road are the most active in the town for ghost sightings and the likes.

FLOATING WOMAN AND THE MOVING CHAIR

I used to work in a bar on Skinnergate. Often we would see the image of a woman on the top floor floating along. Also in the morning when we would be setting up, we found a chair was always moved to the top floor over night. It was a spooky place when you were working there on your own.

THEY ALL FLOAT

I used to work at a pub on Northgate doing the books. And when I was there a young woman often floated up the stairs and past me. But whenever I turned around to see where she went there was no sign of her. I never found this frightening though.

In the 1970s my friend's parents ran the same public house on Northgate. When I visited I remember feeling a definite presence on the stairs to their living quarters.

When I worked there something in the cellar used to shift stuff around and the tap hammer was never in its place. In the past the cellar was used as a makeshift mortuary when there had been an explosion nearby. In the bar, the barmaid's hair used to get pulled. And once I saw a phone and glass fly off a shelf when two barmaids were arguing. Five other people saw this too. One night the landlord let everyone out and was trying to usher out one persistent customer.

He protested, "Why do I have to go when he is still drinking?"

Then he indicated towards the back bar. He was adamant there was someone else there and described a man leaning on the bar drinking. The landlord had to give him the full tour to convince him the bar was empty. Once convinced, the man became as white as a sheet then legged it. He never asked for a stoppy back again!

THE HAUNTED ONES

I have a story to tell. Some family members and I worked as cleaners at a bank on High Row. And every night at least one of us would encounter the supernatural. We have heard loud footsteps coming from the vault and noticed white mist moving up and down the stairs. The mist was often seen by staff during the day too. Once I got locked in the toilets when no one was on the floor at the time! And we often had our bottoms pinched! Things would float through the air at us. We would watch items levitate off the desks and counter and then hurl towards us.

They say the spirits are the founders of the bank Jonathon Backhouse and his mother. The backstairs that leads to their living quarters has a very creepy and oppressive feel to it. This may be due to the fact that Mrs Backhouse fell down those stairs and died. When finishing for the night, we would turn the lights off behind the counters and run to the front door in darkness. I could never have worked there alone at night! It is one creepy place, especially in the dark.

MISCHEVIOUS GHOST BOY

My partner lived in a house off North Road for a short while. I used to stay and as I worked back shifts and he worked during the day, I used to be there on my own. When on my own I could sense something was there. I could hear the buttons on my mobile as if being played with. Also, the landing light would switch back on through the night when we had definitely turned it off.

The strangest thing happened when my parents picked me up one afternoon in the car. My younger brother was waiting in the rear seat. I ran back in to get something leaving the front door wide open. When I came out, my brother (who was about seven) was getting distressed in the back of the car. He began shouting at me to not leave the little boy in the house on his own!

He was saying, "He's there sat on the chair! Don't leave him alone!"

Well, that confirmed it to me straight away. I was glad when my partner moved out as I had said all along there was something in that house. And looking back the things that happened were child-like, such as lights getting switched on and the fiddling about with my phone.

WAKEY, WAKEY

When I first moved into a house off Corporation Road, my children told me they kept seeing ghosts. And I believed them as I once saw a little boy in Edwardian dress leaning against a chest of drawers in the bedroom. Every night something would shake us awake. Every time it happened it was always 2 am and it would be freezing even though the heating was full on.

Not long before we moved out I was shaken awake (it was the dreaded 2 am again.) My son was ill, so I had to stay in his room in

23

case he was sick. So I lay still, feeling nervous. Then something started to bounce up and down on the foot of the bed. I felt it was the spirit of a child. Anyway, I started to shout, "Go away, go away and leave us alone." It stopped. But then, suddenly, a poster on the bedroom door was peeled off and thrown in my direction. I have never felt so scared in all my life; I can tell you.

Another time my daughter (who was staying over from university) was woken up by something nipping her. She never stayed over after that! I heard from one of my old neighbours that when we moved out the workmen doing alterations used to stay overnight and always downstairs. I'm tempted to ask the new owner if they are having problems but I don't want to scare them!

WAKEY, WAKEY THREE DOORS AWAY

I spent a lot of my childhood at an aunt's house which is three doors away from the house in the previous story. And this house was most definitely haunted too. As soon as you walked in the bathroom, there was a huge negative feeling and the taps would turn themselves on. My Gran once confronted it when it was turning the taps on and off and it stopped. I saw many figures out of the corner of my eye too. As I say it did feel like a negative force, but there was also a good one. Once whilst everyone was asleep, my aunt was shook awake by a small boy who pointed to my cousin's room. My aunt ran to check on him and he was choking on his vomit!

A LIFE DRAINING HOUSE

I lived in a house off North Road years ago. It was a house share with a mate. Anyway, as time went by, I became more and more depressed. I lost my job because I couldn't get out of bed. I felt like I was having my life drained from me. The front room near the door had a chair with books on it. The house was part furnished and the front room had a heavy feeling to it. My room was above it. Frequently I would come home and find that the gas ring on the cooker was on. My mate and I put it down to our stupidity. But it happened two more times! We moved out pretty fast. It was far too creepy that house.

SPIRIT BOY OF THE RIVER SKERNE

I've got a fair few stories to tell. Apparently, I am sensitive to this stuff, and it runs in the females in my family. Anyway, I was around five years old and walking into town with my parents and siblings. The part of the river behind what was MFI has a big willow tree and when I looked over, there was a little boy sat on the ledge playing with the water opposite. He was wearing red shorts and a blue vest top with white edging and had brown/dirty blonde hair. I remember wondering how he got down there and where his parents were. I asked if I could play with the little boy in the river and they said there wasn't a little boy there! I looked back and pointed and as I pointed; he looked at me and disappeared. I kept telling my parents that he was there and my mother smacked my bum for making up stories (the sensitivity skipped her.) I've never been able to find anything out about him and wondered if anyone knew anything as it has bugged me ever since.

SOMETHING EVIL

We lived in a house just off Duke Street. One night my mother was poked in the eye, and my brother woke up with something shaking the bed. Every time we went in to the bathroom; there were coins left on the toilet seat. My mam once went to see a fortune teller. He told her to stay out of the bathroom; there was something evil there and to be careful. In the end my mam moved as it was awful and had a horrible energy to it especially on the landing near the bathroom.

I did some research on this house in census returns and found that one previous occupant was an accountant! SC.

MIRROR SPIRIT

My aunt lived in a house on Greenbank Road. She moved in when I was about seven. It always felt strange in that house, like someone was watching. We often talked about ghosts. It was as if we sensed something was there. One night in my cousin's bedroom, which was on the top floor (maid's quarters once over) we were sat on the bed with the door ajar. The door began to open slowly and in walked a

Victorian maid who sat at my cousin's dressing table, looked in the mirror, saw our reflections then disappeared!

I do think there was more than one spirit though. My aunt's dogs would be just sat then run to the corners of the room barking and it would go freezing cold. Once, when I was about seventeen, me and my aunts were talking about ghosts when a massive brass horse flew off the shelf between us. Also, the house had bells in all the rooms and in the back dining room the bell would shake for which room needed assistance. Sometimes the bell would shake to show someone was at the front door, but no one was ever there. My cousin said he saw a man and my aunt saw several spirits. Most people don't even believe me when I tell them.

GHOST CAT

I was driving down Crosby Street about half past midnight. Before I got to the crossroads with Lowson Street, my boyfriend said, 'Did you see the ghost cat?' I asked 'What cat?' Apparently there was a white cat sat bolt upright in the middle of the road wagging its tail. Seemed strange for a cat? It never moved or flinched and I would have run straight over it if had it been real. I saw nothing, but he was adamant it was there. He even got out and looked. There was definitely no cat! It was strange and not the kind of comment he would usually make.

HELD BY AN UNKNOWN FORCE

They say that there is a ghost of a woman who haunts a guest house near the Denes. She is said to have been killed outside on the road many years ago. Her apparition has been seen at the top of the staircase by the manager. Poltergeist activity has also been reported there. Items in the kitchen were moved about overnight, even lights would turn themselves on. And the manager was once 'held' at the top of the staircase by an unknown force!

MY NIGHT VISITOR

My upstairs TV turns on and off and sometimes we hear sounds like someone is walking about upstairs. My boyfriend has felt something touch him and worst of all my son talks to someone in his room. He calls him Garrett and says he comes to see him at night. Once I was in the shower and I could hear my son talking to him in the other room. He hasn't spoken to him for a couple of months now though.

UNWANTED VISITOR

I was talking to someone yesterday whose friend lives near the cemetery off North Road. Her three year old talks to someone that's not there too! Seems to me like the house is full of unwanted visitors!

DISAPPEARING LADY IN THE NIGHT

When my dad was younger, he lived in Alnwick Place. One night he was walking home along Haughton Road after being to Albert Hill Club. As he got towards St. Andrews Church, he noticed a woman, dressed in fine clothes but not too unusual, walking in front. Usually, he would have cut through the churchyard. But as she went that way he decided against it. She hadn't seemed to notice him and might get worried he was following her if he did. He hurried round the long way to the other side (interested to see who the well-dressed woman was walking alone at night!) But no sign of her at all, even further up the road. It still spooks him to this day.

A SCARY FEELING

My family and I have moved into an old house off Haughton Road. There are a lot of strange things going on. We have a lamp in the hallway that's placed on the floor every night (we have it on a table.) We hear footsteps and doors closing upstairs. The living room handle has turned on its own. And the TV unit doors have slammed shut with the handle left swinging. There's such a scary feeling about this place.

LAUGHTER AND SNEEZING

Does anyone know any stories or legends about houses in the North Road Area? Recently moved here and have heard a child's laugh and a man sneeze in the house when I am in on my own.

ROTTING FISH

I have had a few events over the years in different places. In 1998 my wife and I moved into a two-bed house over the Denes. We saw the house once and after a quick look round we rented it without getting a feel for the place. After the hustle and bustle of settling, we realized we had made a mistake as there was an ever present feeling of gloom and despondency. And even though it was a mid-terraced house we could never get the rooms warm despite having the heating on full. We always felt as though we were being watched. Our cat would sometimes stand at the bottom of the stairs looking up and do a low growly meow. We heard footsteps in the main bedroom even though we were downstairs, and occasionally a smell of rotting fish on the landing. We lasted twelve months as we were tied into a long tenancy otherwise we would have left a lot sooner!

THE LADY IN RED

One day when I was about sixteen, I walked my young cousin to Longfield School. After I had dropped him off, I walked back home through North Road Cemetery. As I started along the path, I noticed a lady up ahead walking on the path in front of me. She was pushing a big pram and had a little boy walking alongside her. I'd say he looked about three years old. I remember the lady was wearing a red coat and looked quite made up and elegant; the little boy wore a cap.

At the time, I did not think they were ghosts or think anything strange about it. But, as we walked up the path, they turned (as if to walk onto the grass where the graves are.) And as I passed where they had turned, they were nowhere to be seen! It was only later that it dawned on me how they were dressed and the style of the big pram that they were not real people! I'm quite a sceptic, but I am convinced of what I saw.

The Raby Hotel, West Row (now the site of the Cornmill.)

The former Backhouse Bank, High Row.

St Andrew's Church, Haughton-le-Skerne.

North Cemetery, North Road.

River Skerne, Stonebridge.

Skinnergate.

LADY IN RED AGAIN

I've lived in Longfield Road for years. I saw the Lady in Red (as I call her) once again in North Road Cemetery near the Thompson Street entrance. I must have been about a hundred yards behind her. I stopped to light a cigarette but by the time I got out of the gate she had gone and I was only about a minute and a half behind her.

GHOST ON THE BRIDGE

When I was younger, we used to go up to North Road Station and I swear one time we saw a ghost on the bridge above North Road itself!

DARK FIGURE

Talking about myths and legends, the saying goes if you drive up North Road at night in the dark passing the cemetery gates you can see a dark figure standing there. Now the figure stands next to the phone box that was installed. We passed those cemetery gates one night and were convinced we had seen something!

A SPOOKY MISUNDERSTANDING

In the mid-eighties an elderly couple lived over the road from me on Lascelles Park. Mr Smith was a nice friendly man who would often talk with my children while his wife was quiet and kept herself to herself. One morning I was looking out of my living room window and saw an undertaker coming out of Mr Smith's house followed by the old lady and another lady. It then dawned on me that poor Mr Smith had died. I felt sad about this as I looked to his wife but saw she was waving and smiling at the undertaker as he went on his way.

That to me was weird. But then thought grief does strange things to people.

The following day, I told a neighbour what I had seen and that Mr Smith had died.

She exclaimed, "Oh my God no! It wasn't Mr Smith who died; it was his wife!

HEAD IN THE GAS OVEN

My boyfriend used to live in a house in the Denes area of Darlington. He would often feel like someone was watching him when he was in the kitchen, usually when he was standing at the sink. One night he was sat on the sofa watching TV alone. The TV remote dropped from the back of the sofa to his lap when it had been on the cushion next to him. Needless to say, he was creeped out and went to bed with the light on.

A few weeks later he was talking to a neighbour and mentioned this strange occurrence. The neighbour then said that one of the previous owners had killed himself by putting his head in the oven and joked he might still be around. My boyfriend laughed it off and didn't think about it until later when he was cooking dinner. You know that feeling of being watched in the kitchen when he was at the sink which I mentioned earlier, the oven was opposite the sink. I find that pretty darn spooky!

NOISES IN THE ATTIC

I grew up on the Red Hall estate in the late 70s to the 80s. It would have been around the time I was eight years old. I remember that house being very active. At night, as I lay in bed, shadows would cross the landing, blocking the light before disappearing. Noises would come from the attic and then movement on the stairs. I seem to remember it was so bad at one time that my mother called the police to look in the attic! The house had a very heavy atmosphere. I used to fall asleep petrified of what I would see if I opened my eyes when I heard noises. It chills me to the bone as I write this and recall those days.

SHADOW CHILD

My friend was driving past the South Park towards Grange Road when she saw a black figure/shadow run out from the entrance of the park and into the road. She had to break the car as she thought she had hit something. She thinks it was the shadow of a child. There was no one there.

I've also heard about this, but many years ago. Two people were driving towards the Grange Road junction, and they saw what they thought was a small child running onto the road. Then the child ran back off the road towards the park gates. But the park gates were locked; it was after midnight!

I also heard on another occasion two fishermen saw a child run onto the same road towards the park gates! It was before dawn as they had set off on a long journey.

VICTORIAN LADY IN THE 21ST CENTURY

About ten years ago, I was on my way to work passing the South Park. It was about five o'clock in the morning, and I was in a car with three other people. A woman in a Victorian dress, hat, and an umbrella started crossing the road. I remember we all looked and watched her walk straight through the railings of the fence and into the park!

WHITE SOCKS

My mate and his wife moved into a house off Yarm Road. When visiting I would describe things I was seeing whilst in the living room. I would see white socks walk down the stairs. Once they got to the bottom, they vanished only to reappear and walk down again! My mate's wife used to see them at the same time. It got to the point where we would sit and laugh as they went down. My mate never saw a thing.

One day I went round and his wife told me the weirdest story ever. She used to work shifts and would crash on the sofa. She woke up one day and was in a street. It was nowhere she recognised, but described it as being a busy Victorian street with lots of people in it. She herself was also dressed in Victorian clothes. She says this happened twice. She also had encounters with a hooded shadow waking her on the sofa and pushing her into it. A few weeks past and my mate and his wife started to argue and both changed. They became depressed and withdrawn, and finally went their separate ways.

A year or so later, I was away camping with the scouts and telling ghost stories late at night. One of the younger scouts told us about his old house and how they moved out because of the spooky goings on. He then went on to talk about the white socks and how his mam used to have dark shadows following her around the house. Low and behold it was the same address as my mates!

A FADING WOMAN

My uncle and I saw a woman sitting in the middle of the field at the South Park near the small tree lined riverside. She had her head in her knees crying all alone at 2 am. We went over to ask if she was okay. All she said was 'Hello?' I ran away but my uncle stayed and as he did, he saw her start to fade away. Then, she was gone. We are not the only people to see this, apparently!

TINKLING IVORIES

My grandparents used to live in a Victorian terrace near Darlington town centre. They would often hear a piano being played upstairs (even though they did not have a piano.) Also, one night they were in bed reading when the door swung open and a black figure rushed towards the bed!

I have conducted some research on this house and was surprised to find that in census records a previous occupant was a piano teacher! SC

TOP HAT AND TAILS

This happened on Firthmoor. It was late summer in the 1960s. The nights were drawing in and three children were playing in a shed in a garden that backed onto the railway. All of a sudden, a man appeared in the shed window. His face was green and looked 'just like a ghoul' one of the terrified children recalls. After what seemed like ages, the man's face disappeared. When the children came out of the shed, they saw him running over the railway towards the woods. He was dressed like an undertaker in top hat and tails they said.

ROAMING THE BEDROOMS

I know a story about a ghost from many years ago. It is safe to give the street name where it happened, as it is now demolished. The ghost of an old woman made her presence known to everyone who lived at this address. She would wander the upstairs at night going from room to room at Whorlton Moor Crescent. The house was number 26. I lived at 24 where the landing windows faced each other, but I didn't see this haunting. I just heard stories from the people who lived there who spoke of someone roaming the bedrooms!

OLD WOMAN AT THE WINDOW

My uncle once lived in a house near the railway station. My cousins told me that their eldest sister was always talking to an old lady in her bedroom, and nobody liked sleeping in that room after she left home. I was also told strange things started to happen. They would come down on a morning, and things had been moved. Odd bits would go missing then reappear days later. Then one morning, they came down to the curtains on the floor and chairs tipped over. From what I was told, they got someone from church to come and try to cleanse the house and that was the end of things.

About ten years later, we had a young lad named Mike working with us. Anyway, one morning he didn't turn up for work but arrived later in the day with a cast on his arm. I asked him what had happened.

He said, "You won't believe me if I tell you."

But I persuaded him to tell us anyway. He said he had been cleaning the windows at his new house and had climbed on to the bay window to clean the bedroom ones. Then he said as he stood up there was an old woman staring through the window at him. It scared him so much he fell off the bay and broke his arm. I asked where he was living and lo and behold it was my uncle's old house!

ALL HALLOWS' EVE IN A CEMETERY

In 2012 on Halloween, a friend and I went ghost hunting. Not very good but we hoped to see something. All in all, if anyone remembers it was a pretty rainy night, but we went anyway. Our first stop of the night was at the West Cemetery off Carmel Road. We parked up around the corner and walked in past the two houses which are now warden offices. All the while, I could see an orange light right just past where the newer graves and my uncle are buried.

I said to my friend, "That orange light is a street light from the road," (looking at Google Maps, I assumed it was coming from Baydale Road.)

We continued down the central road. Now and then we stopped to shine our torches about to look at all the old headstones. We approached what I knew to be the crematorium. Suddenly I saw a ball of orange light come out of a tree about five feet from where we stood.

I stopped in my tracks and said out loud, "Stop, the spirits don't want us in here tonight."

My friend turned around and said. "Ok, But why?"

I replied, "No idea. But I get a very unwelcome feeling after seeing that light drop from the tree I think we should leave."

We walked back towards Carmel Road talking in whispers, looking back now and then. I still think they didn't want us there, even though we went to reflect on our lost loved ones.

SUICIDE MAID

When I was at college, I did a work placement in a nursery up the West End of town. The staff used to tell stories of a spooky nature. One story I remember concerned the playhouse upstairs in the room that had a working bell in it. At night when all the children had gone, it used to ring on its own, even when there was no one around to press it! They said it was the ghost of a maid who had committed suicide by jumping out of the attic window.

A BABY'S CRY

About twenty years ago I lived with my mum, dad and sisters in a house over Blackwell. It had a horrible feeling to it. I had the attic room, and in it I would have the most vivid horrible dreams of ghosts stopping me getting to my parents for help. We would hear a baby's cry from the attic if we were downstairs and doors shutting by themselves. My mum also had what we could only describe as an out-of-body experience. It only happened to her in that house. I was so pleased when we moved away.

ELIZABETHAN GHOST?

Anyone seen a figure dressed in what I can only describe as sixteen century clothing walking along Newton Lane? It has been sighted between Walworth and the Acorn Dairy.

WHO PUT THE LIGHT ON?

I live in a house off Woodlands Road not far from the fountain. It's an old house 1920s I would guess. Last week, my partner came out of the bathroom and walked into our bedroom. About five seconds, later we heard the light click back on as we have a pull cord light. We both went to check, and the light was back on. She definitely turned it off as I heard it. I am a rational person and have looked for an explanation but can't find one.

HAUNTED TWIN

We moved to a house near Parkside the same year as we got married in 2006. We were the first people to occupy the house. It was a nice place with great neighbours and a lovely atmosphere. In 2007 we found out we were going to have a baby, then we found out it was going to be twins! When the twins were born, we struggled, but as they reached six months old everything changed. It all became a lot easier, and we settled into a nice routine. Yet it was now we started to notice other little things. The twins would be giggling at nothing and looking away from us. Doors would be open that we thought we had closed and little things would go missing and turn up in obvious places.

One evening I was going to check on the little ones. I went into the hall and put my foot on the first stair and looked up. From this point I could see into my son's bedroom. My heart about jumped into my throat, for standing next to the cot was a woman! From what I remember she was middle-aged with black hair to her shoulders, wearing a salmon coloured jumper and a black skirt. This sighting happened several times over the following months. As well as this sighting, my wife would hear a female humming a lullaby during the night. This scared her a lot but never bothered the children. My wife would go and check on them, but the humming would stop and no one would be there. I never heard it but have no doubt she did.

As the children got older, they began to toddle as little ones do. It was the summer of 2009. We had patio doors leading out into the garden and the children were playing in and out of the house. My daughter toddled from the living room towards the garden carrying her blanky, gabbling on. I was washing up and saw her pass me with her brother, or so I thought. Two minutes later, I went in the living room to get my coffee and there was my little boy playing with his toys quite happily. Who then was with my daughter? I rushed into the garden to see my daughter playing on her own. A shiver ran down my spine. I saw the ghost boy several times after that, always with my daughter and always mistaking him for my son.

South Park gates, Parkside.

Yarm Road.

West Cemetery Chapel, Carmel Road South.

The River Skerne with Stonebridge in the distance.

ROTTING FLESH

My brother-in-law and his fiancée live in a house over Pierremont where strange things happen. The telly would be facing the wall in the morning. Locked doors would be open again. Jewellery would be laid out under the bed, and windows all open. A visiting dog was so spooked it took them an hour to catch it as it ran away into the Denes. The weird happenings seem to follow my brother-in-law around the house. Horrendous rotting flesh smell in his bedroom one minute, then a strong smell of roses and house plants shaking! Any idea what may be going on?

TOO SCARED TO GO TO SLEEP

I live in a house over Springfield and I fear to be alone there. The dogs glare at nothing and bark at the stairs. I often hear noises like loud bangs or footsteps going up the stairs. Once, I woke up in the morning to the sound of a woman wailing. But I was too scared to go downstairs to where the noise was coming from, so I stayed upstairs. I am aware that other people in the house hear these things but they don't often discuss it. There must be a history to this house. I am too scared to go to sleep without the television on in case I hear something.

TRESPASSER OR GHOST?

Excavations at Red Hall in the 1960s revealed that the area had occupation going back to the 13th century. The hall was surrounded by a medieval moat. During demolition of the hall, a figure was seen looking out of one of the upper windows. Not unusual you may think? Maybe it was a trespasser having a look around? Well, who or whatever it was, must have been levitating because all the floorboards and joists had been removed two weeks prior!

FREAKED OUT

My son had a strange experience in the church grounds of Elm Ridge whilst at the nursery. He said he saw people in black running into each other and disappearing then coming back and doing it again. They were very fast, and he said they all had the same face. The staff told me when I picked him up that they were freaked out because he swore it was true. Yet, he wasn't fazed by what had happened as he was so young. We have never forgotten about it and even now, years later he still says that's what he saw.

The nursery he went to is part of an old house. So we did a bit of research. Our research turned up a group of Quaker men stood in black outside that house posing for a photograph. Perhaps they liked to play outside sports, and some energy was being replayed. Whatever was going on, it still makes us think to this day.

LIGHT A CANDLE AND SAY A PRAYER

When I was living in a house off Neasham Road, there were many periods of supernatural activity. Bath taps would turn full on in the middle of the night. Phones that were being charged would switch off at the wall. One time the sitting room light fell out of the ceiling right at my feet. After my son and I saw a figure in the bathroom, I got a clairvoyant to visit. She told me a man had hung himself in the house and would not leave. I got a priest out, and it stopped for a couple of weeks. Another psychic told me to light a candle and say a prayer and ask them to go to the light. After that the activity ceased.

SPOOKY GOINGS ON

I'd very much like to hear if anybody knows the history of the area I live in over Branksome. I often have spooky goings on here. We have heard footsteps on my laminate flooring in the dining room of an evening. Both cats are outside and me and my boys are sitting in the living room. The house is always cold too. My smoke alarm often sets itself off in the middle of the night for 10-15 seconds then stops as quick as it starts. I had this checked by a fire inspector about four years ago. The batteries in it were fine, no dust, and it was in good working condition. He even asked if I had a ghost!

Just now as I've been standing preparing tea, my kitchen door has opened by itself. Yet my eldest son is upstairs, the cats are both outside, the doors and windows are all closed and the heating is on. So there is no draught coming from anywhere. I think much of Branksome used to be farmland but I'm not sure, and as far as I know the house was built in the 1960s.

NOT THE ONLY ONE LIVING HERE

I lived in a house off Willow Road. It was a small two bed terrace with an en-suite bathroom linking the two bedrooms. I always had a feeling I wasn't the only one there, but it never bothered me and whoever it was didn't upset my dogs either. I had been living there for about eighteen months and came into a bit of money. So I decided to move to a bigger property as the house was too small.

The weekend before I moved, I was relaxing in the bath. Laid back with my eyes closed something told me to open them. I did, just in time to see a wall tile coming straight at me. If I hadn't opened my eyes, it would have hit me in the face. When I was talking to the next-door neighbour, she told me no one ever lasted in that house longer than six months. All the previous tenants had been women. I had been there eighteen months with no disturbances until I was moving out. I often wonder if whoever lived there must have liked me and got upset when I was moving.

NEW YEAR'S EVE FRIGHT NIGHT

When I was thirteen, I stayed at my friend's house off Woodlands Road for New Year's Eve. While her parents popped to the pub, we stayed behind to prepare a buffet for when they came back with friends. We were in the kitchen when the door into the breakfast-room slammed shut. The door handles were those round porcelain ones with flowers painted on them. And as we looked at the door handle, the flowers started to move as the handle turned from the outside. We flew to the back of the kitchen where the phone was on the wall. My friend picked up the phone but there was no dial tone. We shot out of the back door, into the yard and out onto the lane. Then we ran around the corner back onto the street and knocked on my friend's neighbour's door. The couple took us in and listened to our hysterical version of events. Then the neighbour phoned my friend's parents at the pub.

My friend's parents came straight back, collected us and took us back to the house. The front door was locked but when we came in the breakfast room door was wide open. My friend's dad dismissed it as hysterical teenage girls who'd more than likely been at the drink. We hadn't. But my friend's mam listened. She was not surprised. She had known there was something in the house for years. I often wonder who was there that night, and what would have happened if we hadn't scarpered.

VICTORIAN CHILD WITH THE FAKE SMILE

I lived in a house off Neasham Road as a child. I moved out after my seventeenth birthday, which would have made it 2004. So we had lived there a long time. I remember being there for my seventh birthday but again we had been there before that. Anyway, I saw a ghost one night-clear as day! A little girl wearing a Victorian nightdress! I woke up in the middle of the night with the strangest feeling. I looked down the side of my bed and there she was, smiling at me. But it seemed like a fake smile, showing her teeth. They were tiny!

My parents told me they saw a man and woman spirit in the house too! My mum woke one night, and she thought it was one of my siblings wanting to get into her bed. But when she looked, it wasn't her; it was a ghost! The house was built in 1913, and from what I'm told (I'm not sure it's true) the house was almost burnt down with a family still in it.

TERRIFYING THE BABYSITTERS

When I was little, our family lived in a house over the Denes and we had some spooky experiences there. I used to tell my parents about an old lady who would frequent the end of my bed of an evening and tell me stories. I also used to terrify my babysitters with such tales. They said that after they put me to bed, they would hear music coming from an unidentifiable source in the house. I had warned them, "If you hear the music start to play come and get me, don't leave me alone." I have no recollection of these events though. My parents and a family friend who babysat me when I was a toddler told me at my eighteenth birthday party.

Also, my dad worked nights. And when my mum was in the kitchen making tea (around 6 pm) she would often feel a presence. And so she would turn around sure she would see my dad entering the room. But there was never anybody there. I don't remember much of living in the house, but the one thing I do remember is the thing that spooks me the most. I remember getting up one morning and sneaking into bed with my mum before my dad got back from his night shift. I could hear my little sister chattering away to someone. My mum seemed a little concerned about this. I said, "It's just our friends that float in through the window," as though it was the most normal thing in the world. Looking back, it gives me chills.

As an adult, my mum told me the sisters who sold us their house had told her it belonged to their elderly mother. She had passed away on the premises and was not found for a few days.

Could this be the source of some unrest? I would like to make it clear that we never felt in danger or threatened in any way during our time in the house. The house has gone up for sale recently though, and I would love to arrange a viewing to see if I can pick up on anything.

SO ANGRY

Well, here's the story of one of my experiences. I'll just skim over the basics. My parents lived on Bank Top a few years back. Dad loved DIY, and the house was a mess. Once he got up to go to the toilet and saw an old woman with long hair in the spare bedroom. He kept quiet about it and then a little while later my Mam saw the same thing and mentioned it to Dad. It transpires a woman died in the house and it took a while for anyone to notice. Basically, it looked like an accident. But it was being investigated.

Anyway, my parents split up, and the house was empty. There was a massive freeze and the pipes burst in the attic. Me and brother-in-law went round to try to stop any further water damage. It was such a state. I mean water leaked everywhere and ruined family items. So, a few months pass. The house is still upside down, but now dryish. I get told I can go and salvage the wooden doors with glass panes for my own house. So off I pop to the house. I go upstairs with my screwdriver and get the funniest feeling I'm being watched. But to be expected nothing. I go to the bathroom, and I think I see something in the mirror in where my Dad saw the old woman. I turn around, still nothing.

So I begin to whistle to myself. Feeling really cold and a bit freaked out, I start unscrewing the bedroom door to the room the old woman was found in. I then notice the replaced floor board from where blood had seeped through the carpet. Again, I feel a bit funny. I get the door off as quickly as I can, take it downstairs and make my way back up. The temperature has now gone freezing and I have goose bumps and the hairs on my neck are all on full flare. I walk to the next door, but it's warped from the water. So I go to the little bedroom. I bend down and notice the temperature has gone up again. I feel more relaxed. I start unscrewing the door and then there is an almighty bang and crash behind me. The temperature drops in a split second and I can see my breath. I turn to look and I swear to God, the attic hatch has opened and the ladders are hurtling straight for my head. I rip the door off the hinge and fly down the stairs and out the house.

To this day, I swear that old lady was angry at the state the house was in. Yet, the woman who lived there previously had mentioned her daughter had seen an old lady in the house too, but had never felt threatened.

FACE AT THE WINDOW

I've always been a non-believer and said I won't believe until I have seen. Well yes, it happened and even now my hairs stand on end when I think about it. I was working behind the bar one night at a club. I was finishing off and cashing up as the security guy walked around checking the doors. All doors were locked and nobody else was in the building. I was just about to lock the bar shutters when I glanced towards the kitchen /restaurant. There is a door between the restaurant and the kitchen that swings but is heavy to push. I saw a face/head at the window looking at me. After my expletive the security guard looked too. This figure stayed for a few seconds then the door started violently swinging about two feet in each direction. We just stood there stunned and to be honest pretty scared. We looked at each other and said someone's in the kitchen. Yet the security guy had checked, and it was all locked. After a few minutes we somehow got the bottle to go in and look. Switching the lights on we saw nobody and everything was locked.

I have to be honest and say this completely freaked me out. If I had been alone, I'd have put it down to being tired or just imagination playing tricks. Well no, maybe I wouldn't. But I think you would go a long way to see two fully grown men as frightened as we were. I have told very few people as I didn't want to alarm the members or staff and this was around two years ago and haven't heard any other reports since.

Apparently it was built on the old railway works and I'm not sure if that has any link. There have been occurrences in previous years of figures seen and cold drafts but I'd always thought it was just peoples' imagination. I now know different!

PADFOOT

When I was a little girl of around eleven years old, I do believe I saw a hellhound in the field behind our bungalow. My dad was the caretaker of Springfield school, and we lived in the school bungalow called 'Rockwell'. This was within the school grounds. One afternoon I was playing in the school field at the back of our place, when from out of nowhere I was suddenly confronted by a large animal. It looked like a cross between a dog and a lion. I was in the RSPCA and liked animals but didn't recognise this as any breed of dogs I had either read about or seen before. The animal looked at me and I stared back in amazement. I then decided to run back to the house and get it something to eat, as it was looking as if it wanted to eat me!

"I'll get you some food," I told it, and turned to do that.

I only looked away for a moment and when I glanced back it had gone. We were in the middle of a large field, so I wondered why I hadn't seen it going away.

On that same afternoon, my aunty from Stockton came to visit us. She gave me ten shillings, something unbeknown (and ten shillings was a lot of money in those days.) She lived on a farm with her family and rarely came through to see us. So we were all quite surprised, but welcomed her warmly and then bid her a fond farewell when she left. Two days later, we were told she had committed suicide the day after her visit to us.

Years later I discovered that the sighting of a large hound called Padfoot (aka The Barguest of Throstlenest) a legendary hound local to my area of town) was a foreteller of death. We were all shocked and devastated when the news came that my aunt was gone.

It was only years later that I heard the story of the ghostly dog which was said to roam the area, and it made me wonder...

FEVER HOUSE

I lived in a former railway house in Hopetown. I know about a family that lived there long ago with a baby boy and a little girl. I also know the little girl died in the house from a fever. The little girl who lives there now plays with this spirit girl and calls her Abigail but a psychic got the name Eve. Also sightings of an old man in uniform have been seen there. I had a friend who lived at the same house too. I went there one night to babysit her eight-year-old daughter as I was a childminder. I also had a two-year-old with me whose mother had been told 'he has the gift'. Anyway, all was going well until I had to change the baby's nappy. This was the conversation I then had with the girl.

"That stinks I'd hate doing that."

"Yes it does smell but if I didn't do it who would?"

The little girl then said, "The man, he's upstairs if you want to meet him he's looking after the children."

As you can imagine, I absolutely shit myself! I told her to stop talking nonsense and brushed it off as kids have wild imaginations! I locked us in the front room as I was petrified hoping the mother would come back soon. We had left the sweeties in the kitchen, so I asked one of the children to run through to get them. To get to the kitchen you must go past the stairs, he's normally good and runs there and back after about a minute I heard this horrendous scream and hysterical crying I ran through to find the child at the bottom step of the stairs looking up. I automatically looked up to the top of the stairs and there he was, the angriest old man I'd ever seen floating on the top of the landing with his finger on his lips telling us to hush. He had a long trench coat with no bottom half and didn't disappear until I had stopped the crying! I was petrified. Luckily, the girl was still in the front room, so I didn't let on that I'd seen him. The children's mother came in not long after and I vanished out of that house!

It was playing on my mind the whole night, so I plucked up the courage to text the mother and ask if she had ever experienced anything and told her why. She immediately wanted to meet up. We met up the next day, and she brought a photograph with her. It was the man I saw in uniform and it was her granddad! We were confused as to why he was so angry. So the mother decided to get psychics into the house to do some investigating and thought it was only right I went! The mother also told me countless other stories about spirits in the home. Psychics came round and explained the granddad was angry because there was too much noise and he was trying to get a spirit baby to sleep upstairs.

The house, as I said earlier, was for men employed by the railway. In what is the eight-year-olds room at the moment was a little girl's of around the age of five. It came out that the father of the little girl brought a fever into the home and the young girl caught it and died. The mother due to this event went on to have mental health issues. To get over the death, they decided to have another baby. It was a boy, and the room was then transformed into his. The mother didn't want a boy and one night he was crying so much that she suffocated him!

Anyway, back to the night the psychics were there. It was just awful. Lights were going on and off, beds were bouncing, and chandeliers were rocking. In the young girl's bedroom, toys were getting played with in front of our eyes! I would never ever go back into that house ever! Ghost hunters have also been in there and caught tons of orbs on camera.

My great Uncle Tom also lived in that railway house. He died many years ago in the back room where he was found. He died of a stroke. He was a lovely kind man with a heart of gold so no need to worry. What is weird is that he used to wear a trench coat, so it must be him!

SEVEN OF SPADES

Okay, here goes. My friends lived in a house over Hopetown way and to say weird things happened would be an understatement. Not one person who visited was left unscathed by the happenings. The first time I visited, three of us were sitting in the front bedroom with the window open and two friends had gone for a walk. About half an hour after they had left, we distinctively heard our friend's voices outside. I heard both of them, whereas the other girl only heard one of the voices. They were so like our friend's voices; we thought they were back but we didn't hear the door go. It transpired that they were miles away and had not returned. We later heard the door, but once again they had not returned.

Fast forward a few weeks and after more strange experiences for the friends who lived there, I was a target again. I was in the bedroom with one of the friends who lived there. We were playing cards when behind me I heard the wallpaper border start crackling like somebody was moving it, despite knowing I hadn't touched it I told myself it was probably just me. But then another thing happened, we were playing Jacks, Twos and Eights and my friend had put down a card. I'd looked over to see what she had put down and my eyes just caught the fact it was a black seven. I knew I had a black seven in my own hand, so I looked towards my hand and I saw the seven of spades. Looking back to my friend's card to double check, I saw she'd put down the seven of spades too and when I looked back to my hand; it was actually the seven of clubs! I knew I'd just been staring at the seven of spades in my hand, because I was somewhat planning my further moves from putting down that card. To say I freaked out was an understatement!

My last experience was walking through the kitchen, when from behind me I distinctively heard a sniffle, despite the fact my friends were in a separate room. But the worst part was it sounded like my friend even though I knew she was in the other room. It seemed like whatever was there, was able to copy the voices and sounds of those around it as well as warp what people saw!

WET WOOLY GLOVES

My mam lived in a house off North Road in the early 1980s and had a strange experience there. She was woken up one night with what felt like someone on top of her pinning her shoulders down with his knees. When she struggled, it felt like hands over her mouth wearing wet woolly gloves. She shouted for her brother who checked the house but there was no one there and all the doors were locked. My mam also knew someone who lived in the house after we moved out, and they said that strange things were happening to them too.

UNSOCIABLE SPIRITS

I would like to tell you some spooky things I've experienced but wish to stay anonymous. I used to live in a house on Harrowgate Hill. I remember we had just moved in, and I had a dog. We had just settled in, and then some strange things started to happen. I had a chair in the corner of my front room and when I sat there I used to become very cold. I put it down to just moving in and it being a strange house. One morning I had come from a night shift and dozed off in the chair. I woke up to someone shouting at me I couldn't make out what they were saying and I couldn't see anyone. I got up, checked the whole of the house but no one else was there except the dog and me. I was very scared, so I went out and returned an hour or so later. Nothing happened for a few weeks after that, so I put that experience down to being very tired.

A few weeks later, my family and I were sat watching telly, while my dog lay sleeping. She jumped up and started growling and barking at the corner of the room. It was as if she was warning us someone was there. Then it went very cold and a massive bang came from the kitchen. We went to look, and every single pan was on the floor! To this day we still can't explain the strange things we saw or heard. I asked a neighbour about the house and she said a couple used to live there and the husband had taken his own life in the front room. This was shortly after his wife had died. My neighbour said they hated dogs and weren't very sociable people. That would explain why my dog wouldn't settle and all the other strange things that happened.

GHOST SOLDIER ON THE STAIRS

The one supernatural experience I'll always remember was when I was a kid. My mam, dad and sister were out, and I was at a friend's house around the corner. I brought him round mine to show him what I'd got for Christmas. While we were in the living room, we heard a noise upstairs. We hurried into the hallway to see who it was, thinking it might have been a family member. But there at the top of the stairs was a First World War soldier in uniform and wearing a full-length trench coat. I turned to my friend to ask if he could see him. But he had already legged it. I looked back around and he was coming down the stairs. That was it, I was off. I've never been so terrified in all my life. The house I lived in was on Whessoe Road (no longer there.)

RELEASED

Does anyone know about the Springfield area before the river went through it? Apparently it was all marsh land. When I moved in a few years ago my two-year-old kept getting wipes out and wiping the air in front of her saying dirty. I invited a medium along to help. She told me my child could see a little girl who drowned in marsh land and she was looking for her dad. The medium then released this little girl to meet her dad again.

SPOOKY BASEMENT

My grandparents moved to a house over the Denes area, where they saw some strange things. Once granddad was in the basement when a group of Roman soldiers marched past him! My mother reported seeing their rocking chair move on its own and there was always an uneasy feeling in the attic.

NON-BELIEVER

My hubby and I lived near North Road Cemetery about twelve years ago. We lived in the house next door-but-one to the graveyard, up at the top of the street. My husband had his very first experience of ghosts in that house. He had never believed in them before. He used to see a youth dressed in Victorian style clothes. The spectre wore a peaked cap, and a fitted jacket belted at the waist and knee length britches. He has gone on to encounter a few since then in various pubs we have had. But that was his first.

RING, RING

This is my main ghost story. I'm trying to figure out the date; it must be the late 1960s. I grew up on Mowden and my friends and I often played around the building sites. I remember the lodge was being renovated at the time. They had also cut down all the trees to build the new houses next to the old house too. It had those wire fences and boarding right around like they do on building sites.

I was there with some mates one day thinking how we could get in. As we peered through the wire fence, we saw a figure in the living room window of the lodge. We couldn't work out how there was anyone in there because the doors were boarded up. As we looked on, it was all very strange. The figure looked like a skeleton or a painfully thin person in grey, answering a telephone. We couldn't see the figure clearly, but the telephone was quite clear. It was similar to one of those Bakelite phones you see in old movies. I don't know why, but we felt the figure was not right and threatening. So we legged it.

Afterwards we talked about what we had seen. So I knew I couldn't have imagined it because my mates' versions were the same as mine. I went back there later and there was nothing in the room at all. No furniture, no telephone, not anything.

SPOOKY SHIFTS

I worked on night security at Darlington Forge and ended up working in the main area. Night times were hairy to say the least on patrols. I once saw a figure one evening, wearing a shirt with sleeves rolled up and a waistcoat; it was a bloke with long sideburns. I just caught a quick glimpse in the torch beam, flicked it back and he'd gone. There were a few orbs on the security feed cams too.

I also worked in a unit behind Darlington Forge. One winter's morning I was getting into my lorry after opening the gates. As I went to close the door, I could see a pair of legs on the other side of the driver's door. It was if someone was standing there. When I looked to see who it was, there was no one there. There wasn't anyone else in the yard at that time except me. It kind of made me dubious about being there on my own after that.

Elmridge Church, Carmel Road South.

Neasham Road.

North Road.

The former Darlington Forge, Albert Hill.

ABOUT THE AUTHOR

Sylvia Clement was born in Darlington and still lives there with her family. She studied at Queen Elizabeth Sixth Form College and also the University of Teesside where she gained a First Class Honours Degree in English Studies.

Printed in Great Britain
by Amazon

37810580R00050